CARS

CONTENTS

CONTENTS

This is a Grandreams Book
This edition published in 2004

Grandreams Books Ltd
4 North Parade, Bath BA1 1LF, UK

Designed and packaged by
Q2A Design Studio

Printed in China

CAR CRAZE

Since very early times, people have constantly devised ways to move from one place to another. The first vehicle that was self-propelled (not drawn by animals) appeared in 1769, when Frenchman Nicholas Cugnot built a steam-powered carriage. It moved at only 5 km (3 miles) per hour.

The Motor Generation

The motor car came of age with the invention of the internal-combustion engine. Its development started in the 1850s. The first petrol-driven engine was perfected by Gottlieb Daimler around 1880. From the 1890s onwards, cars fitted with small steam engines were used in the United States.

Then, in 1908 came the Ford Model T – a landmark creation. It was the first car to be mass-produced, which made it available and affordable for ordinary people. Since then, the craze for cars has continued and the motor car remains a source of fascination to many.

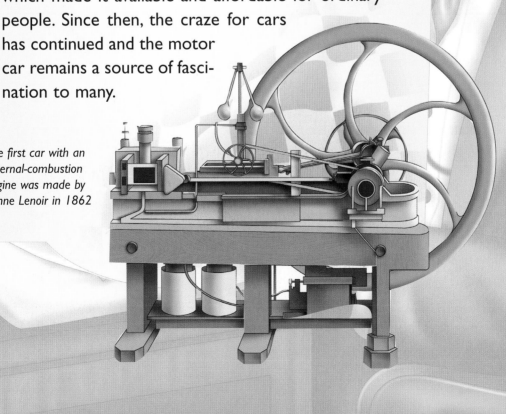

The first car with an internal-combustion engine was made by Etienne Lenoir in 1862

CAR CRAZE

Which was the world's first car to be sold commercially?

A two-seater tricycle called Benz Motorwagen was the first commercial car. It was made in 1885 by Karl Benz, a carriage builder.

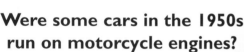

The big-wheeled Benz Motorwagen looked somewhat like a horse carriage!

Were some cars in the 1950s run on motorcycle engines?

The German BMW Isetta, a microcar, was powered by a motorcycle engine. Microcars are nicknamed 'Bubblecars' because of their round shape and large windows.

Which car was called the 'Hummingbird'?

The earliest motorized London taxi was called the 'Hummingbird'. The 1897 Bersey electric car got its name because it made a humming sound.

Which was the first car to be built in large numbers in a factory?

The Ford Model T by Henry Ford was the world's first mass-produced car. All the car parts were made in large numbers, so that many cars could be assembled at the same time. This became known as the production-line method.

Launched in 1908, the Ford Model T was affectionately called 'Tin Lizzy'

When was a petrol-run car first driven?

In 1870, Siegfried Marcus of Austria first drove a car on petrol. It was so noisy that Marcus was banned from driving it again.

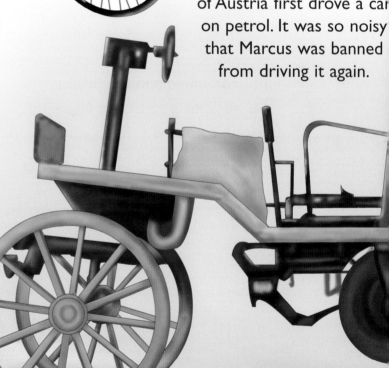

The Marcus car was the first to use gasoline as a fuel

How do modern factories make millions of cars in just a few days?

Modern factories use Ford's production-line method to manufacture cars. Some machines weld metal parts together, some attach fittings and others spray paint.

What was the special feature of the Peugeot Bebe?

The Peugeot Bebe, first produced in 1913 in France, had the smallest engine of its time. The car, which was extremely popular for its day, was built with a four-cylinder, 855-cc engine.

FACT BOX

☐ Early cars were very expensive because their instruments were assembled by skilled craftsmen. Seats were lined with thickly padded leather to prevent bumpy rides.

☐ In 1862, French engineer Etienne Lenoir invented the first car engine run on coal gas.

☐ In the 1930s, the German government conceived the idea of an inexpensive 'people's car'. That was how the Volkswagen came into being. Designed by Dr. Ferdinand Porsche on Hitler's orders, its unusual shape earned it the nickname 'Beetle'.

In German the meaning of Volkswagen is 'people's car'

CAR CRAZE

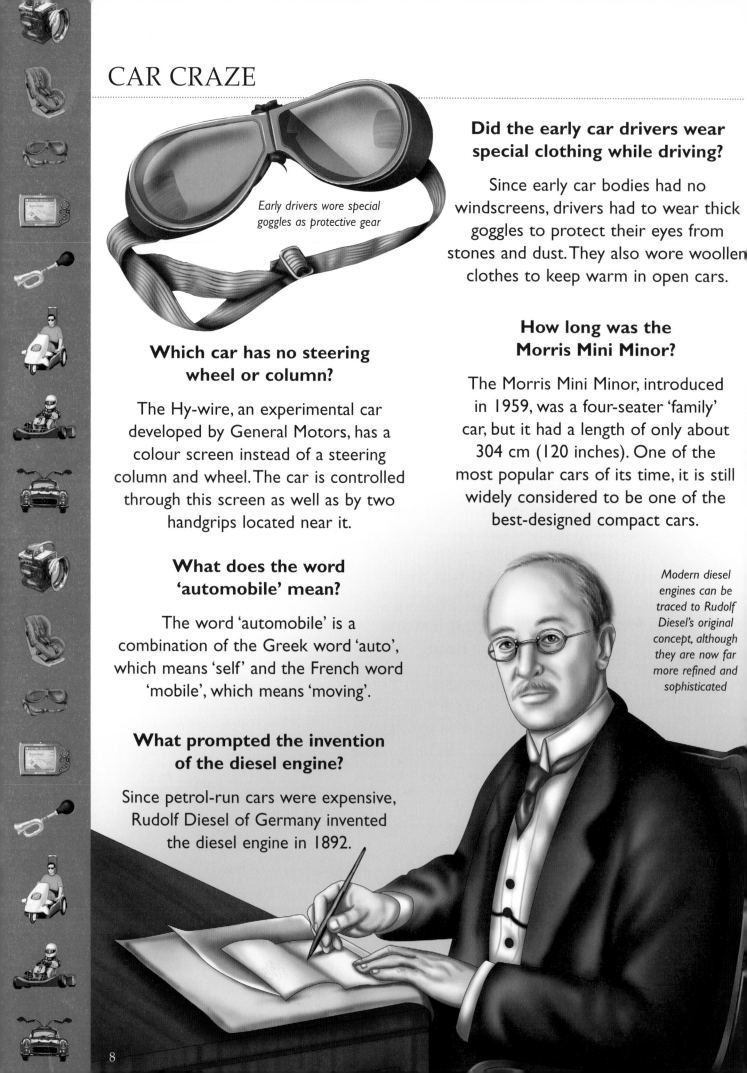

Early drivers wore special goggles as protective gear

Did the early car drivers wear special clothing while driving?

Since early car bodies had no windscreens, drivers had to wear thick goggles to protect their eyes from stones and dust. They also wore woollen clothes to keep warm in open cars.

Which car has no steering wheel or column?

The Hy-wire, an experimental car developed by General Motors, has a colour screen instead of a steering column and wheel. The car is controlled through this screen as well as by two handgrips located near it.

How long was the Morris Mini Minor?

The Morris Mini Minor, introduced in 1959, was a four-seater 'family' car, but it had a length of only about 304 cm (120 inches). One of the most popular cars of its time, it is still widely considered to be one of the best-designed compact cars.

What does the word 'automobile' mean?

The word 'automobile' is a combination of the Greek word 'auto', which means 'self' and the French word 'mobile', which means 'moving'.

What prompted the invention of the diesel engine?

Since petrol-run cars were expensive, Rudolf Diesel of Germany invented the diesel engine in 1892.

Modern diesel engines can be traced to Rudolf Diesel's original concept, although they are now far more refined and sophisticated

TYRE TALE

In the beginning, cars needed a lot of clear space in order to travel over bumpy and rutted roads. So they used large wheels. Modified from horse carts, the wheels used to be very heavy too. They were usually made of iron and wood. Today, wheels are manufactured from alloys or compressed steel. They are not only durable and strong, but lightweight and compact as well.

This early, heavy wheel has iron spokes and a wooden rim

Comfy Wheels

An early type of tyre was made of solid rubber. In spite of giving a hard ride, without any cushioning effect, it rarely suffered from punctures and was therefore quite popular. Later, pneumatic (air-filled) tyres – offering a softer and more comfortable ride – were introduced. The first such tyres were very narrow, with an inner tube that had very high level of air pressure. Later still, a wider 'balloon' tyre was developed. It had a lower level of air pressure and was less rigid than the first pneumatic tyres. The result was a smoother ride!

This early tyre is made of solid rubber, unlike the modern air-filled rubber tyre

9

TYRE TALE

Grooves increase the grip of a tyre and help prevent a car from skidding and sliding on the road

Why do tyres have an uneven surface?

Tyres have raised pads, small grooves and water-draining channels on their surface so that they can grip the road well. A smooth tyre tends to skid as it moves.

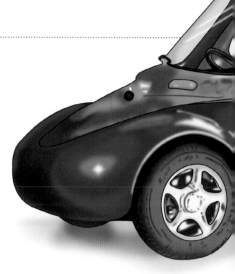

Do all cars have the same type of tyres?

Different cars have different tyres depending on their size and shape, as well as the type of roads and weather conditions of a particular area. For instance, there are winter tyres for cool regions.

Why are tyres so important for a car's performance?

Tyres come in contact with many different types of road surfaces, such as rough, smooth, wet, dry and icy. Tyres are very crucial to both safety and performance because if they do not grip the road securely and steadily, a car cannot stop, turn corners, or speed up efficiently.

Why do cars skid on wet roads?

As a car speeds down a wet road, water forms a film around the tyres. This can lift the tyres off the road surface, causing the car to skid. To prevent this, tyres have drain channels to push the water away from under the tyre as it rotates.

Who is the Michelin Man?

The Michelin Man is the well-known trademark of the Michelin tyre company of France. It features a 'man' – made entirely out of tyres – juggling a ring of tyres over his head.

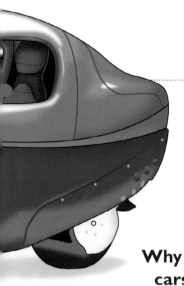

A bubble-shaped, three-wheeled car that did not remain popular for very long

Why are three-wheeled cars not popular?

Most modern cars are four-wheeled, with a wheel placed at each corner. This evenly distributes the car's weight on the road.

Are ordinary tyres suitable for racing cars?

Racing-car tyres are made of very hard rubber mixtures to cope with heat generated from the car's speed on a racetrack. Ordinary tyres would melt in such conditions. Sometimes, racing cars use smooth tyres ('slicks') to reduce friction and achieve extremely high speeds.

Racing cars use special tyres made of extremely tough rubber, as well as smooth 'slick' tyres without grooves

FACT BOX

□ Modern sports cars have wheels made of really light alloys. Earlier, these cars usually used wire-spoke wheels, which could take the strain of the high speed and sharp turns taken by the car.

Wire-spoke wheels are light, tough and stylish

□ Rubber tyres with inner air-filled tubes were prone to punctures. Bad-quality roads littered with pebbles and stones, or even a pin lying in the car's path, would cause the tubes to burst. Modern technology has now made it possible to make tubeless tyres.

□ Dr. John Boyd Dunlop invented pneumatic rubber tyres in 1888. The air-filled tube absorbed the impact of the car's contact with the road, giving a comfortable ride. The Dunlop tyre was first used in bicycles.

11

TYRE TALE

The grooves of a tractor tyre are especially deep, so that the vehicle does not slip and slide while moving over mud and slime

Why do tractors have high, deeply grooved tyres?

A tractor tyre's grooves are designed to grip the slippery mud of farms. The height of the tyre enables easy passage over obstacles, while the width spreads the weight of the tractor on the ground.

Why is 'hydroplaning' dangerous?

Hydroplaning happens when a car is driven over a puddle of water and the water is subsequently not squirted out rapidly enough from the tyre. The car gets lifted off the ground and remains supported only by water. This is dangerous because there is no traction and the car can easily go out of control.

What makes white clouds appear around a car's rear wheels?

When a driver accelerates and then brakes suddenly, the wheels spin very fast. The tyres, rubbing against the ground, burn with the heat of friction and release white smoke.

What is a 'severe snow use' tyre?

Tyres designed for use in conditions of heavy snow are manufactured and tested in a special way because they need to have grooves with superior gripping power. The tyres are tested on snow and then certified with a special 'severe snow use' icon.

How are rubber tyres made strong?

Rubber tyres are strengthened with an internal network of cords and webbing made of materials such as nylon and steel.

A CAR RIDE

There are many things that contribute to the look, feel and handling of a car. Automotive technology is now so advanced that cars are constantly being updated, modified and reinvented.

Honk! Honk!

One device that allows a car to make its presence felt is the horn! Early cars had a wide array of horns, such as air-bulb horns and 'trumpet' horns. The Clarion Bell was a 'hands-free' gong that could be operated by the driver's foot. It allowed the driver to use both his hands to control the car.

A driver could press this warning bell with his foot

A car horn with an air pump

A Big Hand

Accessories are an important aspect of any car and this was true for early motorists as well. Before flashing indicators became a standard feature, there were some unusual gadgets that served the purpose of signalling. One such was a mechanical hand that was attached to the car door. The driver rotated a knob built into the dashboard in order to position the hand for various signals.

A CAR RIDE

Why does the Lamborghini Diablo have a 12-cylinder engine?

The Lamborghini Diablo is a very powerful car that needs a lot of energy to accelerate quickly. Its 12-cylinder engine burns much more fuel than an ordinary 4-cylinder car, thus helping it generate the required energy.

What is a convertible?

A convertible is a car with a roof that can be folded back. The hood can be fixed over the car during winter, or when it rains.

The Lamborghini Diablo is one of the most sought-after cars

Why do cars have multiple gears?

Cars have several gears to achieve different combinations of speed and force. The first and second gears provide more force than speed. The fourth gear is used for driving on flat roads, while the fifth is for high speed. Cars may have up to six gears, depending on cost, use and design.

Why is it unsafe to drive a car with wet brakes?

Disc brakes function due to friction between brake pads. Since water reduces this friction, a driver may lose control of the vehicle if the brakes are wet.

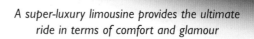

A super-luxury limousine provides the ultimate ride in terms of comfort and glamour

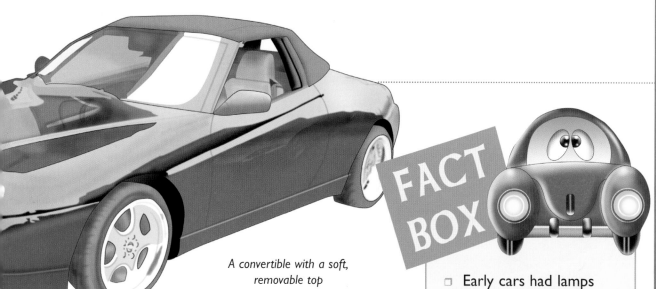

A convertible with a soft, removable top

What kind of horns did the early cars have?

A rubber bulb attached to a brass tube was the horn for most early cars! When the driver squeezed the bulb, air travelled through the tube and made a sound as it came out from the other end.

Are there any car brakes that are used only after the car is parked?

Parking brakes, operated by the handbrake lever, lock the rear wheels when the car is standing still.

Early cars had lamps on one side of their bonnets. These were lit by burning oil or gas. Oil was usually carried in a small container at the bottom of the lamp.

An early car lamp that ran on oil or acetylene gas

In modern cars, wind-shield wipers are designed and manufactured with a capacity of 1.5 million wipes.

The first functional car radio was named Motorola because it was a kind of 'moving radio' (radio in motion). Motorola went on to assume the name of Galvin Manufacturing Corporation and is now a world-famous brand.

What makes luxury cars, such as the limousine, bump-free?

Cars use suspension systems to prevent bumpy rides. Luxury cars like the limousine have the Selective Ride Control (SRC) Suspension System to provide an extra-smooth ride.

A CAR RIDE

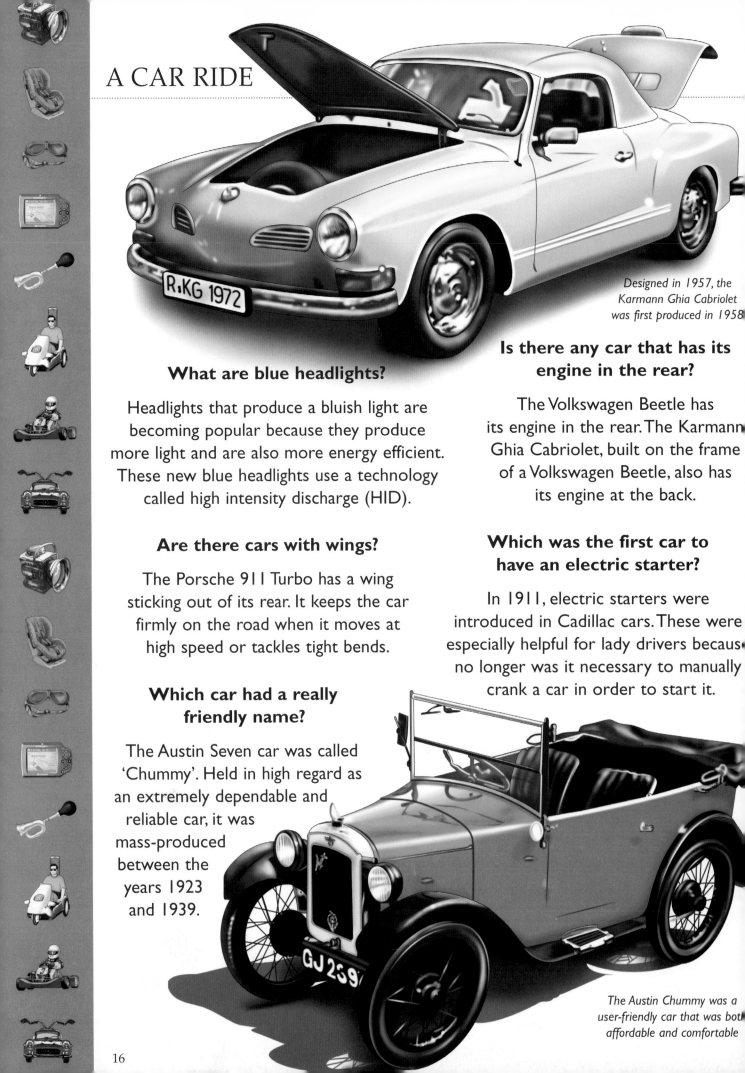

Designed in 1957, the Karmann Ghia Cabriolet was first produced in 1958

What are blue headlights?

Headlights that produce a bluish light are becoming popular because they produce more light and are also more energy efficient. These new blue headlights use a technology called high intensity discharge (HID).

Are there cars with wings?

The Porsche 911 Turbo has a wing sticking out of its rear. It keeps the car firmly on the road when it moves at high speed or tackles tight bends.

Which car had a really friendly name?

The Austin Seven car was called 'Chummy'. Held in high regard as an extremely dependable and reliable car, it was mass-produced between the years 1923 and 1939.

Is there any car that has its engine in the rear?

The Volkswagen Beetle has its engine in the rear. The Karmann Ghia Cabriolet, built on the frame of a Volkswagen Beetle, also has its engine at the back.

Which was the first car to have an electric starter?

In 1911, electric starters were introduced in Cadillac cars. These were especially helpful for lady drivers because no longer was it necessary to manually crank a car in order to start it.

The Austin Chummy was a user-friendly car that was both affordable and comfortable

CAR RACE

Racing cars symbolize sheer velocity, thrilling adventure and intense competition. These awesome speed machines now come in the latest ultra-light materials and some are so low-slung that they seem to be almost touching the ground. These features, along with extra wide wheels and hugely powerful engines, enable the cars to attain amazing speeds. Often termed as 'aerodynamic', the sleek and streamlined bodies of racing cars help to reduce the drag from the air rushing past the car.

Suction Skirt

Racing cars are designed to make use of air pressure. Initially, most of them had a kind of 'skirt' that almost reached the ground. This created a vacuum beneath the speeding car which was filled by the surrounding air. The resultant suction effect helped to keep the car firmly on the ground. 'Skirts' were later banned because these encouraged drivers to race at extremely high – and risky – speeds.

On a Bend

Grand Prix circuits have sharp bends specifically to restrain excessive speeds that may lead to dangerous accidents. These are also a test of the drivers' skills.

A car racing around sharp bends is a thrilling sight!

CAR RACE

The Ferrari F1-2000 weighs about 600 kg (1,323 pounds)

What is special about Ferrari's F1-2000 engine?

The Ferrari F1-2000 with its V10 engine is a smaller, more compact and more powerful version of the typical Ferrari engine. Michael Schumacher drove it to victory in October 2000.

When was the world's first car race held?

The world's first long-distance car race was from Paris to Bordeaux in 1895. Emile Levassor won it in 48 hours but was later disqualified.

Are sports cars successful racing cars?

Sports cars, or roadsters, can be driven in races as well as on ordinary roads. Their bodies and engines are usually tested for toughness at the Le Mans 24-hour race in France. The Jaguar D Type won the Le Mans 24-hour race four times between 1953 and 1957.

What is the most popular kind of track racing?

Formula One racing, or Grand Prix, is the most popular kind of track racing. The first Grand Prix was held in France in 1906.

The first Grand Prix car race held in 1904 included cars made by Mercedes, Fiat and Renault

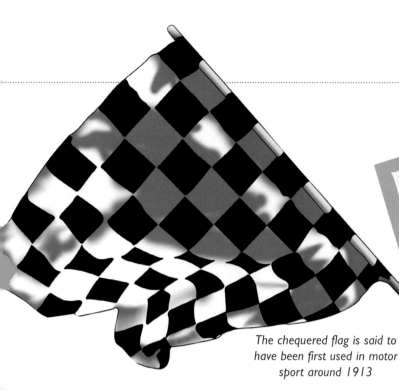

The chequered flag is said to have been first used in motor sport around 1913

What is common between chess and car racing?

The black-and-white chequered pattern associated with a chessboard is also a symbol of motor racing. It is waved when cars cross the finishing line after a race.

In which car race is the winner awarded a quart glass bottle of chilled milk?

The winner of the Indianapolis 500 race is presented a quart glass bottle of chilled milk, along with a flower-studded wreath. Louis Meyer, the 1936 winner, started the tradition when, following his mother's advice, he drank some milk after the race!

Which car race has cars starting at different times and following difficult terrain?

Rally driving follows a difficult path that is divided into special stages, like mud-filled roads, snow patches and slushy rivers. The cars start at different times but follow the same route, with a time limit for crossing each stage. The car with the fastest overall time wins.

FACT BOX

□ Rear-view mirrors were invented in the 1920s. Prior to this, a mechanic seated in the car used to warn the driver about another vehicle trying to overtake him.

The rear-view mirror made it unnecessary for a mechanic to sit with the driver and guide him

□ The Indianapolis Motor Speedway racetrack, with a tar-and-gravel surface, is also called the Brickyard because, until 1961, it was partly paved with bricks. With over 250,000 seats, it is the world's largest seating facility.

□ A drag race is like an athlete's sprint run – short and fast. Cars may reach a speed of up to 400 km per hour (249 mph) on the approximately 402 metre (1,319 foot) long track!

19

CAR RACE

When did Ferrari first win a world championship event?

Ferrari had its first-ever F1 victory when its driver, Froilan Gonzalez, won the RAC British Grand Prix at Silverstone in 1951.

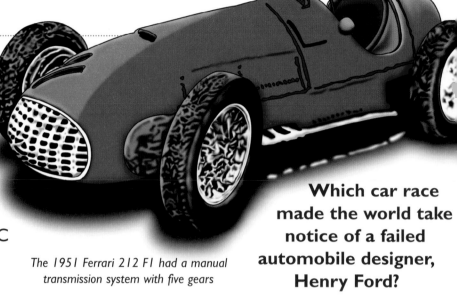

The 1951 Ferrari 212 F1 had a manual transmission system with five gears

What are hairpin bends on a racetrack?

Sharp bends on racetracks are known as hairpin bends. As the cars speed towards the bend, drivers have to brake hard and then accelerate again after crossing the bend, without letting the car skid or spin.

When was the first Grand Prix held?

The French Grand Prix, held at Le Mans in 1906, was the world's first race to be given the title of Grand Prix. The winner drove a Renault at about 101 km per hour (63 mph) to win the approximately 1,127 km (700 mile) long race.

Which car race made the world take notice of a failed automobile designer, Henry Ford?

In 1901, at a car race held at a horseracing track in Michigan, Henry Ford – in his 26-horsepower, self-designed car called Sweepstakes – defeated noted race driver Alexander Winton. The race built Ford's reputation as an automobile designer. He opened the Ford Motor Company in 1903.

What do we mean by a constructor?

The chassis (framework) builder of a Formula One car is called a constructor. The F1 World Championship title for Constructors was introduced in 1958. Racing teams are known by the names of their constructors.

Engineers, designers and scientists make use of computer-aided design technology to create as well as test racing cars

FULL SPEED AHEAD

The first cars were run by steam. During the late 19th and early 20th centuries, these were produced by several manufacturers. Among them were the twins Francis and Freelan Stanley, who built the 'Stanley Steamer'. The steam car was popular in its time, but by 1929 it was no longer in production.

Electric Energy

The electric car was developed in Europe during the 1880s. Although hugely popular, it was unable to run efficiently if the speed exceeded 32 km per hour (20 mph). Moreover, the battery had to be recharged after every 80 km (50 miles) of travel.

Petrol Power

Petrol-run cars appeared around 1862. By 1885, both Karl Benz and Gottlieb Daimler had built gasoline-powered cars. The year 1901 saw what is considered to be the first mass-produced car – the famous 'curved-dash' Oldsmobile, developed by Ransom E. Olds.

This 1902 electric Studebaker could seat two passengers and had a collapsible top

SPEED AHEAD

Which British Royal Air Force pilot drove a car at a speed faster than that of sound?

RAF jet pilot Andy Green was the first person to go supersonic on land. In 1997, he drove the Thrust SSC, powered by two jet engines, at about 1,228 km per hour (763 mph).

The Thrust SSC set its supersonic land record on the Black Rock Desert in Nevada

Which racer named his car 'La Jamais Contente', meaning 'never satisfied'?

It was Belgium's Camille Jenatzy. He had made two failed attempts to break Comte's land speed record of 62.78 km per hour (39 mph). Then, in 1899, Jenatzy's electric car reached a new record speed of 106 km per hour (65.86 mph).

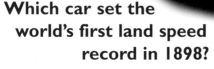

Which car set the world's first land speed record in 1898?

In 1898, a Jeantaud electric car, driven by Comte Gaston de Chasseloup-Laubat of France, set the world's first land-speed record when he reached 62.78 km per hour (39 mph).

Which speed-record holder's father had set nine land speed records himself?

Donald Campbell's father, Malcolm Campbell, was the holder of nine land speed records.

What kind of engine was used to run the first car to reach a speed exceeding 1,000 km/hr?

In 1983, at Nevada's Black Rock Desert, Richard Noble drove his jet engine-powered car to become the first to touch a speed of some 1,018 km per hour (633 mph).

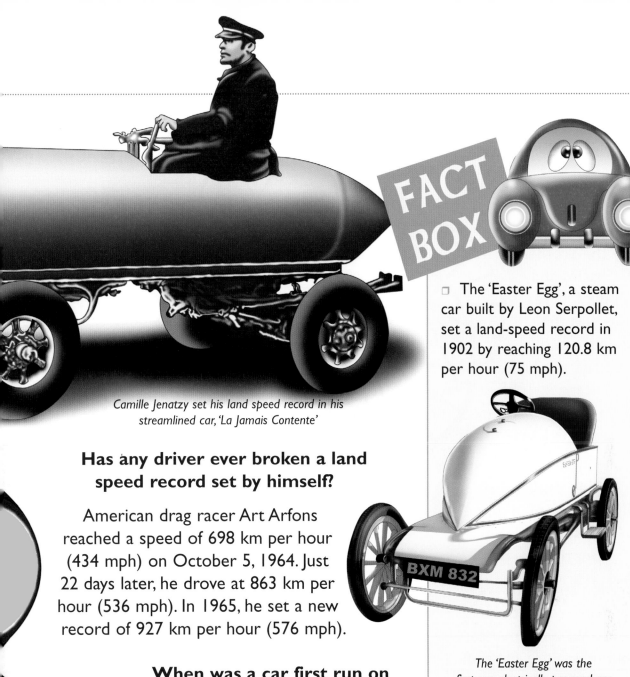

Camille Jenatzy set his land speed record in his streamlined car, 'La Jamais Contente'

Has any driver ever broken a land speed record set by himself?

American drag racer Art Arfons reached a speed of 698 km per hour (434 mph) on October 5, 1964. Just 22 days later, he drove at 863 km per hour (536 mph). In 1965, he set a new record of 927 km per hour (576 mph).

When was a car first run on an aeroplane engine?

On March 11, 1929, the Golden Arrow, powered by a Napier-Lion aeroplane engine, set a land speed record of 372 km per hour (231 mph) at Daytona Beach, Florida.

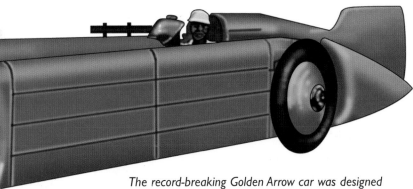

The record-breaking Golden Arrow car was designed by J.S. Irving and driven by Henry Seagrove

FACT BOX

□ The 'Easter Egg', a steam car built by Leon Serpollet, set a land-speed record in 1902 by reaching 120.8 km per hour (75 mph).

The 'Easter Egg' was the first non-electrically powered car to set a land speed record

□ The world's first two land-speed records were set at The Flying Mile at Britain's Brooklands racing track.

□ The Castrol Motor Oil Company, set up by Sir Charles Wakefield in 1899, awards a trophy to drivers who break land speed records. Englishman L.G. Hornsted became the first winner when he drove his Benz at 200 km per hour (124 mph) in 1914.

SPEED AHEAD

Which car won the first driving race?

A superior version of the first gasoline-powered car – built by the brothers Charles and Frank Duryea – was the winner in the first car race held in Chicago in 1895. The car was driven by Frank Duryea.

The Duryea car was manufactured by Duryea Motor Wagon Company

What makes salt flats a popular place for setting land speed records?

Salt flats, which are prevalent both in Australia and America, provide a long, flat and hard surface for cars to reach a high speed quickly.

Who established the first automobile factory in Italy?

In 1899, Italian industrialist Giovanni Agnelli founded Fabbrica Italini Automobili Torino (Fiat) – the first automobile factory in Italy.

What kind of record did Louis Chevrolet set?

In 1905, Louis Chevrolet set a speed record of 109 km per hour (68 mph) during his first race. He later designed and built the first Chevrolet car in 1911.

Which was the first experimental car designed by Henry Ford?

Henry Ford created his first experimental car in 1896. He called it a 'Quadricycle' because it ran on four bicycle tyres.

Built on a steel frame, the Quadricycle was fitted out with an electric bell in front and a bicycle lamp on the side

AN OFF-ROAD DRIVE

The all-terrain vehicle (ATV) was built as a utility-and-recreational vehicle. It is used for purposes as varied as farming, forestry, law enforcement, adventure tourism, trail riding and camping. For people who enjoy the outdoors, the ATV allows them to venture into rugged, 'off road' places.

Modern ATVs are usually four-wheelers. Most of the early three-wheeled ATVs were withdrawn in the mid-1980s because they were not considered safe. Modern ATVs are designed and built to very strict safety standards, especially with regards to brake performance and vehicle stability.

Big and Bigger

ATVs come in different shapes and sizes. Some, like the Triton Predator, have as many as eight wheels for extra power and strength. Some others are relatively small and particularly safe for young drivers. They have a reduced speed capacity and such features as a restraining strap that allows a supervising adult to stop the machine.

An ATV has special features such as an extra high clearance and very large powerful wheels

AN OFF-ROAD DRIVE

What are half-tracks?

First used during World War II, half-tracks are part-trucks and part-tanks meant for military use. They have tracks (like those of a tank) at the rear for travelling over broken roads and debris. The wheels at the front help them move easily.

The half-track is lighter and easier to manoeuvre than a full-sized military tank

How do we better know the GP (General Purpose)?

The GP, developed by the U.S. Army at the start of World War II, is known to us as the jeep. With its strong engine and tough body, the jeep was originally designed to travel on roads damaged by warfare.

The jeep can tackle the toughest of driving conditions

How did the all-terrain vehicle develop?

The idea of an all-purpose, all-terrain vehicle developed from the jeep as well as the British Land Rover. Its special features include high ground clearance and extra-strong suspension, braking and transmission systems.

What special features can be seen in an ATV meant for safari?

A safari ATV has an extra-tough roof rack (on which a tent can be pitched) and an observation roof hatch (that can be raised for viewing wildlife).

How are victims of wars or natural disasters treated in remote places?

Aid agencies reach out to patients in mobile hospitals – specially adapted trucks fitted with medical equipment.

What was the top speed of the first Lunar Rover?

The top speed of the first Lunar Rover was about 11 km per hour (7 mph).

☐ The Lunar Rover, carried to the Moon in 1971 by Apollo 17, was car-like, open-roofed and electric-powered.

The Lunar Rover was fitted with such high-tech equipment as a satellite dish

Which vehicle was built on the same lines as the jeep?

The British Land Rover, made by the Rover Company in the 1940s, was modelled on the jeep. It was built for farmers so that they could easily travel across undeveloped country roads.

The tough and reliable Land Rover is popular both as a working vehicle and as a fun car

☐ Off-road vehicles, or all-terrain vehicles, can easily drive across rough terrain, be it mud, desert, or stony ground. They often stand high off the ground and have sturdy bodies with large tyres.

☐ Off-road races are organized globally. The best-known is the 11,000 km (6,835 mile) Paris-Dakar-Cairo Rally, first held in 1978.

AN OFF-ROAD DRIVE

How do golfers travel around the golf course?

Golf karts, or golf buggies, are small, lightweight vehicles that carry golfers and their heavy golf clubs around the course. Driven on batteries, they cannot carry more than two people.

Golf buggies usually have a high roof but no windscreen or windows

Why is the Lunar Rover called the 'ultimate off-roader'?

The Lunar Rover's Moon Mission involved moving over an extremely rocky surface that also had a deep layer of sand. It had to work in an environment where there was neither air nor gravity and experienced extreme temperature changes. It also had to be extra strong because there were no repair facilities up there!

What were the special features of the 'Moon Buggy'?

The 'Moon Buggy', as the Lunar Rover was called, was constructed mainly of aluminium to keep it light and portable. It was 3 m (10 feet) long and 1.8 m (6 feet) wide. It had special wheels made of piano wires woven together.

Where was the first go-karting event held?

A go-kart is a small indoor-racing car with wheels. It was first made by Art Ingles using a lawnmower engine. The first go-karting event was held in 1956 in a shopping-centre car park in California in the U.S.

Why are ordinary cars not suitable for driving on a beach?

Usually, three-wheeled vehicles (tricycles), fitted with light-weight balloon tyres, are used for driving on a beach. The wheels of an ordinary car can sink into the wet sand.

Go-karts provide plenty of fun and thrills

COLLECTOR'S CARS

Collector's cars are those that have made a mark in some way. These cars have stood the test of time in terms of their design, unique features, or their place in the history of cars.

Some cars are admired as symbols of innovation; some are cherished for their sheer good looks; and many others have a special place in the hearts of collectors. One of the most-loved cars is the Volkswagen Beetle. It still inspires fond feelings and is held as one of the ultimate style statements!

Classic Veterans

The oldest type of collector's cars is popularly referred to as veteran cars. These include cars made before the year 1905. These cars are extremely rare and are the prized possessions of their owners. They need constant maintenance and care.

Cars made between 1905 and 1919 are also called Edwardian cars because King Edward VII was the monarch of England during that time.

A classic Edwardian heritage car

COLLECTOR'S CARS

What was special about the Rolls Royce Silver Ghost?

First built in 1906, the Rolls Royce Silver Ghost was a large, expensive car that could be altered to suit the buyer's needs. It was last built in 1925.

How did the Rolls Royce get the name 'Silver Ghost'?

During its time, the Rolls Royce Silver Ghost was hailed as a marvel of engineering. Its supremely elegant silver body and noiseless engine (which was compared to ghost-like quietness) inspired the name 'Silver Ghost'!

The Rolls Royce was often referred to as the 'best car in the world'

How are collector's cars classified in terms of a specific era?

Collector's cars usually refer to those that were made years ago. These include veteran cars (made before 1905), Edwardian cars (1905-19), vintage cars (1919-30) and classic cars (1930-70).

Are antique cars ever driven by their owners?

There are tours and rallies in which antique cars in working order can participate. Veteran cars participate in a London-to-Brighton car run every year.

Why did the 1955 Cadillac Fleetwood have two carburettors?

The carburettor of a car feeds the fuel-air mixture into the cylinder, where it is burnt to release energy. The Cadillac needed two carburettors because it used more petrol.

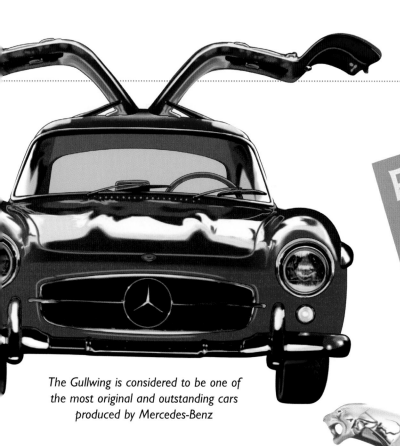

The Gullwing is considered to be one of the most original and outstanding cars produced by Mercedes-Benz

Which car, nicknamed 'The Gullwing', was built by hand?

The 1954 Mercedes-Benz sports car was built by hand. It was the first car to have its doors opening upwards from the roof, looking somewhat like the wings of a seagull! Only 1,400 such cars were ever made.

Which 1968 car remains one of the world's fastest cars?

The 1968 Ferrari 365 GTB4 Daytona, with a top speed of about 281 km per hour (175 mph), remains one of the world's fastest cars.

The 1968 Ferrari 365 GTB4 Daytona enjoys the status of an iconic 'supercar'

FACT BOX

▢ Jaguar cars carry the emblem of a leaping jaguar. The third largest animal in the cat family, the jaguar is a symbol of power and speed.

The Jaguar emblem

▢ Clubs such as the Antique Automobile Club of America (AACA) and FIVA (Federation Internationale des Vehicules Anciens) have collectors of antique cars as their members. The clubs help members meet each other.

▢ When the 1957 Ford Thunderbird was first sold, buyers were given both hard and convertible tops so they could use whichever one they wanted. The car won a Lifetime Automotive Design Achievement Award in 1998.

COLLECTOR'S CARS

The Jaguar XK 120 was acclaimed for both its performance and looks

Which 1949 British car is highly valued by collectors?

The 1949 Jaguar XK 120 sports car, with a high speed of 193 km per hour (120 mph), is one of the most sought after of collector's cars.

How long was the Cadillac Coupe de Ville?

The Cadillac Coupe de Ville, a classic American car of the 1950s, was 6 m (18 feet) long. Its exceptionally long fins extended through the length of the car and made it one of the most recognizable and innovative cars of its time.

Which classic car created history with its smallness?

At a length of merely 3 m (10 feet), the 1959 Morris Mini Minor was the most compact car of its time. It became known for its remarkable performance.

Which American vintage car has its exhaust pipe coming out of the front bonnet?

The SJ Speedster model of the Duesenberg car has the exhaust pipe coming out of the bonnet. It is a collector's favourite and also very rare – only 36 cars were ever built!

Why did cars have fins?

In the 1950s, American cars were designed and built as showpieces of luxury and beauty. One typical feature of these cars was the fin, which was first introduced around the late 1950s. The fin got larger and larger, until it became an outstanding style feature.

The Duesenberg SJ Speedster is a prized collector's car that is highly valued for its quality, design and sense of luxury

CARS WITH A DIFFERENCE

The process of designing and building a car is not only very expensive, but also involves a lot of research and effort. Nowadays, computers play a very important role in the process. Computer-aided design (CAD) is used by the car industry to come up with innovations in styling and performance.

Cars are constantly being reinvented with new features and unique concepts. In fact, there is a whole new breed of cars referred to as 'concept cars' which are specifically designed to be different. These cars are a combination of distinctive style features, creative technology and glamour.

O for Orange

Some concept cars are designed for specific purposes. One such was the 'Orange' car, made in 1972-74. A specially created chassis gave the car its remarkable shape – that of an orange! Used only for advertising purposes, the 'Orange' was mainly found in the United Kingdom, France and Germany. It is believed that there is one that is still being used in South Africa.

The 'Orange' is a striking example of a customized vehicle built for a specific purpose

XLG 9837

CARS WITH A DIFFERENCE

Can a car's roof be stored in its boot?

The Lexus SC 430 was the first car to have a retractable (foldable) hard roof. When a specific button is activated, the roof folds up and is stored in the boot, which opens and closes automatically in response.

The Lexus SC 430 is a sports coupe that can be turned into a convertible within 30 seconds

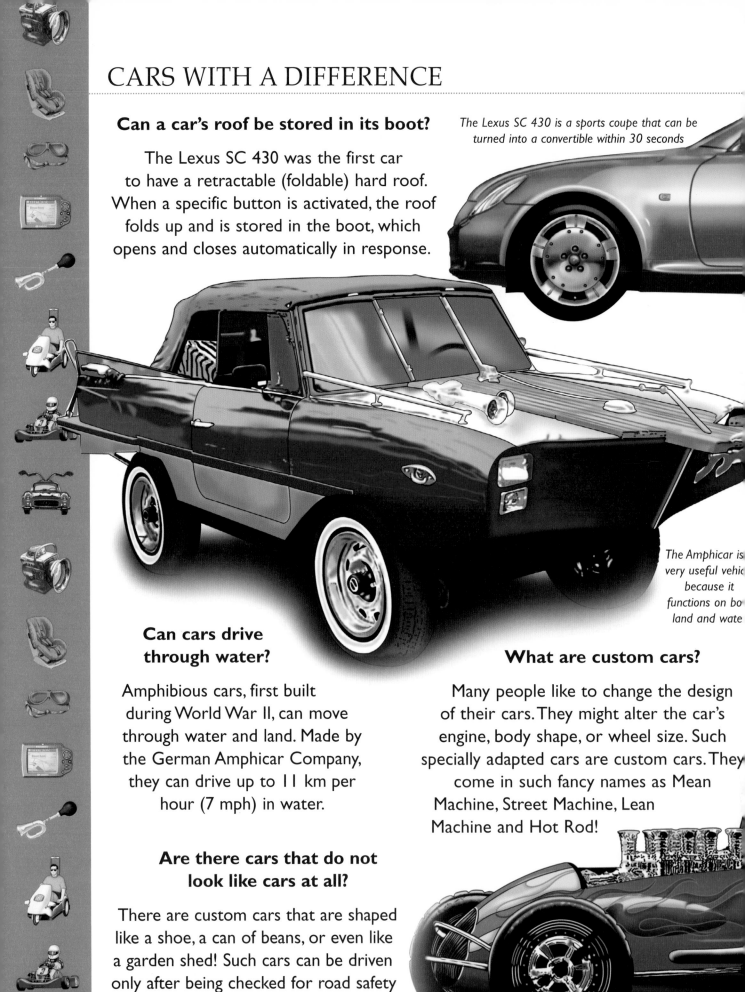

The Amphicar is a very useful vehicle because it functions on both land and water

Can cars drive through water?

Amphibious cars, first built during World War II, can move through water and land. Made by the German Amphicar Company, they can drive up to 11 km per hour (7 mph) in water.

Are there cars that do not look like cars at all?

There are custom cars that are shaped like a shoe, a can of beans, or even like a garden shed! Such cars can be driven only after being checked for road safety and properly fitted with a horn, headlights, indicators and safety belts.

What are custom cars?

Many people like to change the design of their cars. They might alter the car's engine, body shape, or wheel size. Such specially adapted cars are custom cars. They come in such fancy names as Mean Machine, Street Machine, Lean Machine and Hot Rod!

Are custom cars used in car racing?

Custom cars are preferred for races in which crashes are more likely to occur. These so-called stock cars may be fitted with turbochargers to pick up speed within a few seconds. Such cars are run in drag races.

What is special about the Dream Truck?

The Dream Truck, originally owned by Spencer Murray, is a custom car that was built in the 1950s. It has fins on its body.

Hot Rods are modified to improve performance and are also seen to reflect an owner's personality

What special features did the Rolls Royce Phantom 3 have?

The Phantom 3 had the same engine technology as that of the aircraft engines produced by Rolls Royce. This super luxury car had special speed-sensing shock absorbers to ensure a smooth and comfortable ride.

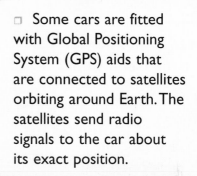

FACT BOX

❑ Some cars are fitted with Global Positioning System (GPS) aids that are connected to satellites orbiting around Earth. The satellites send radio signals to the car about its exact position.

The GPS tracking system provides cars with information about location and routes

❑ American car company General Motors is developing a car that can transform from a saloon car to a pick-up truck following a voice command by the driver!

❑ Kit cars can be made even by people who are not experts. There are kits containing all the car body and engine parts. These pieces can be put together by following an instruction booklet.

CARS WITH A DIFFERENCE

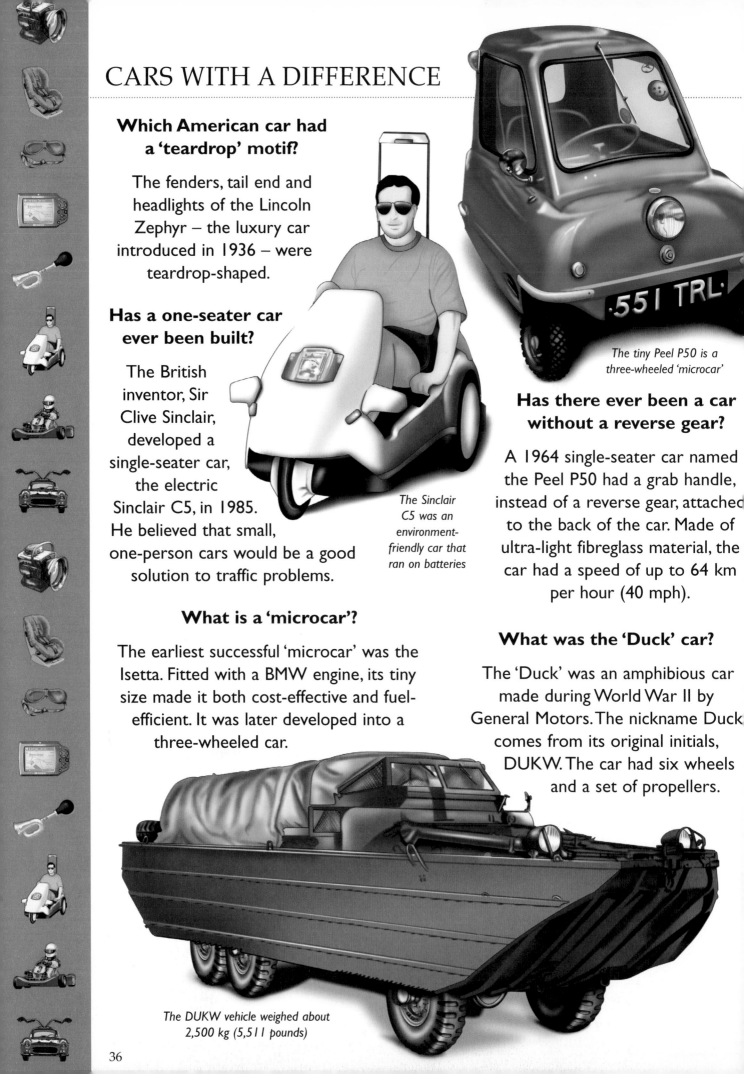

Which American car had a 'teardrop' motif?

The fenders, tail end and headlights of the Lincoln Zephyr – the luxury car introduced in 1936 – were teardrop-shaped.

Has a one-seater car ever been built?

The British inventor, Sir Clive Sinclair, developed a single-seater car, the electric Sinclair C5, in 1985. He believed that small, one-person cars would be a good solution to traffic problems.

The Sinclair C5 was an environment-friendly car that ran on batteries

What is a 'microcar'?

The earliest successful 'microcar' was the Isetta. Fitted with a BMW engine, its tiny size made it both cost-effective and fuel-efficient. It was later developed into a three-wheeled car.

The tiny Peel P50 is a three-wheeled 'microcar'

Has there ever been a car without a reverse gear?

A 1964 single-seater car named the Peel P50 had a grab handle, instead of a reverse gear, attached to the back of the car. Made of ultra-light fibreglass material, the car had a speed of up to 64 km per hour (40 mph).

What was the 'Duck' car?

The 'Duck' was an amphibious car made during World War II by General Motors. The nickname Duck comes from its original initials, DUKW. The car had six wheels and a set of propellers.

The DUKW vehicle weighed about 2,500 kg (5,511 pounds)

36

A SAFE DRIVE

The car industry is constantly involved in research and development to make better, safer and more efficient cars. Modern cars have to meet many standard safety requirements, such as the strength and rigidity of side doors for ensuring passenger safety. Collapsible steering wheels reduce the danger of injury through crushing or piercing if there is a head-on collision.

A Dummy's Life

A crash-test dummy is an artificial figure made from materials that are very similar to the structure and composition of the human body. A crash dummy's spine, for instance, is made from layers of rubber pads and metallic discs so that it is almost like the actual human spine. A dummy has the very important function of simulating, or mimicking, a human being during the trauma of a car crash. Hundreds of cars, along with crash dummies, are deliberately wrecked in order to collect valuable data about the effects of collisions and accidents. All this is done to improve safety features that will protect the occupants of a car during an accident.

Crash-test dummies are used in mock car crashes to analyse data about the effects of car collisions

A SAFE DRIVE

Traffic signals (1914 period)

What led to the introduction of traffic signals on roads?

Traffic signals were introduced to control the traffic flow. The first electric traffic light was installed in Ohio, U.S., in 1914.

What is crash glass?

Crash glass is a special type of safety glass used in cars. Even in the event of an impact, the glass does not break up into sharp and jagged pieces. It goes through a special 'tempering' process that enables it to break up into small, rounded pieces.

Who was the first driver to be punished for driving under the influence of alcohol?

In 1897, George Smith, a taxi driver in Britain, was asked to pay a fine of one pound for drunken driving.

What purpose do air bags serve in modern cars?

Air bags first appeared in the 1980s. They inflate when the car collides with something, acting as life-saving cushions by protecting passengers from being thrown forward.

What is the most common method of traffic calming?

Traffic calming means slowing down traffic speed. Building speed breakers (bumps on the road) is the most common method to achieve this.

Which traffic law aimed at preventing road accidents was prevalent until 1904?

A law passed in the late 1800s required every car to have someone walk in front of it with a red flag. The driver was thereby forced to drive slowly, while the red flag warned people to move out of the car's way!

What are the safety guidelines for a child seat?

The normal safety recommendation is that a child up to four years of age should use a child seat. For a 4-8-year-old, a booster seat should be used.

A child seat protects children from injuries during accidents or abrupt braking

FACT BOX

□ Car mascots have been declared illegal because they are dangerous to pedestrians in an accident. The Rolls Royce mascot, a winged figure, folds down backwards into the bonnet in an accident.

The famous Rolls Royce winged mascot is known as 'Spirit of Ecstacy'

□ Speedometers were introduced in cars in 1901.

□ Most roads in the early 1800s were made of stone and wood blocks, which gave a rough ride. John MacAdam innovated a smoother surface in 1819 by coating roads with a hard layer of tiny stones.

The Red Flag Act of 1865 made it compulsory for a car to have two drivers, with one person on foot carrying a red flag in front of the car

39

A SAFE DRIVE

Why do seat belts need to be replaced after a crash?

In most major accidents, seat belts get stretched to the maximum. The components in a seat belt that maintain the belt's tautness are usually meant for one-time use only.

How does an air bag inflate?

An air bag has a sensor that triggers inflation when there is a collision. The inflation occurs because the air bag system pro-duces a large amount of nitrogen gas through a chemical reaction.

A seat belt is an essential, life-saving safety feature

What is the 'crumple zone'?

Many modern cars have a 'crumple zone' in the front section. This area is designed to absorb crash energy generated during a frontal collision. The body of the car 'crumples' in a controlled way, so that the effect of the crash energy is lessened and the passengers are protected.

How are cars tested for strength?

Car engineers make sample cars and conduct standard tests by hitting them against powerful robot vehicles. This helps to identify the weak points in the car's bodywork and make modifications accordingly.

Which invention was inspired by a cat's eyes?

In 1934, Percy Shaw, a British road repairman, invented Catseyes, or glass reflectors, to aid drivers by night. The idea struck him when he braked suddenly in thick fog to avoid a cat whose eyes were glowing in the dark.

Accident involving the 'crumple zone'

CARS AND THE ENVIRONMENT

There are millions of cars all over the world and each car has the capacity to be a source of air pollution. In recent years, there has been a lot of effort to reduce air pollution and clean up the environment. Governments all over the world have made laws and regulations aimed at ensuring that the problems of environmental pollution are addressed. With so much concern and awareness about the dangers of pollution, car manufacturers and users have also become sensitive to the issue.

Battery Power

The electric car is an environmentally friendly solution to air pollution. This is being seen as the car of the future, because it will help to conserve limited resources such as petrol and also reduce increasing levels of toxins and poisonous gases in the air. It has an electric engine driven by a battery-powered controller. The difference between an electric and a gasoline car is that in an electric car the source of power comes from rechargeable batteries.

An electric car provides a practical solution for conserving energy resources because it does not use petrol as fuel

CARS AND THE ENVIRONMENT

Cars pollute the air when they let out exhaust fumes full of toxic gases

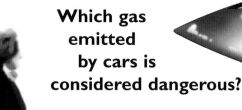

Which gas emitted by cars is considered dangerous?

Cars, while burning fuel, emit waste gases like carbon monoxide. Scientists believe that this gas traps other harmful gases in the atmosphere, making it warm. Global warming might cause glaciers to melt and low-lying areas to submerge under water.

Do electric cars help reduce air pollution?

Electric cars do not depend on energy released from burning fuel and, hence, do not emit any harmful gases. They are powered by batteries that store electricity and can be recharged easily with electric plugs. An electric car can travel almost 160 km (100 miles) after its batteries are charged.

What is the biggest risk involved in transporting oil from oil reserves to petroleum refineries?

Oil is transported in large ships from oil reserves to refineries for the extraction of petrol. If the ship sinks or leaks, oil seeps into the sea, forming a layer on the water's surface. This layer, called slick, may cause many sea creatures and birds to die.

How can old, discarded car tyres be utilized?

Car tyres are discarded once their surface pattern wears off, making them too smooth to grip the road. By shredding tyres into small rubber chips and melting them, asphalt for covering roads can be derived.

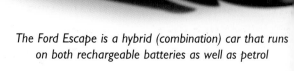

The Ford Escape is a hybrid (combination) car that runs on both rechargeable batteries as well as petrol

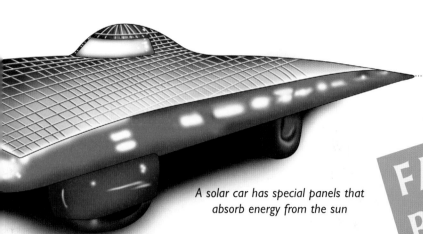

A solar car has special panels that absorb energy from the sun

Can solar energy be tapped to run cars?

Cars run on solar energy were first developed in the 980s. A solar-powered car, Solar Trek 1, was driven by Hans Thostrup and Larry Perkins across some 4,084 km (2,538 miles), from Perth to Sydney in Australia.

Is it possible for a car to run on air?

An experimental car that can run on compressed air, instead of petrol or electricity, is being developed. The compressed air is contained in tanks under the car and can be refilled when necessary.

What is the Escape HEV?

The Escape HEV, made by Ford Motor Company, is a hybrid car designed to run on a combination of petrol and electric batteries. The vehicle, unlike electric cars, will be able to travel long distances.

CARS AND THE ENVIRONMENT

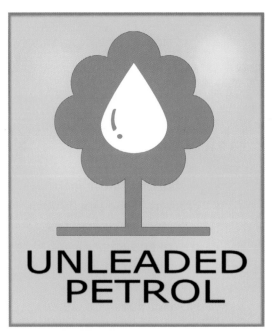

Petrol pumps now provide unleaded petrol for promoting a pollution-free, cleaner environment

What is a catalytic converter?

A catalytic converter treats harmful wastes – such as hydrocarbons and carbon monoxide – produced by the exhaust from a car, converting them into harmless substances. The catalytic converter contains precious metals like palladium and platinum to aid in the process.

Why do we need an alternative to petrol for running cars?

Fumes from petrol-driven cars settle over the earth as thick layers of smog (smoke and fog). Smog causes many respiratory diseases. CNG (Compressed Natural Gas) is a good alternative to petrol, producing 20 per cent less emissions.

Why do cars use 'unleaded' petrol?

Unleaded petrol (that is, petrol that does not contain the metal, lead) is a safer fuel because it has a less toxic effect on the environment. Research has revealed that lead is a very dangerous air pollutant.

Why do traffic policemen wear masks?

Traffic policemen wear special anti-pollution masks to reduce the effects of breathing in exhaust fumes from vehicles. While directing traffic they are constantly exposed to high levels of pollution.

What is an oxygen sensor?

An oxygen sensor is part of a car's emissions control system and is located in the exhaust pipe. It helps a car's computer to calculate exactly how much oxygen needs to be drawn in by the engine and reduces wasteful intake.

A pollution mask filters out the harmful toxins produced during heavy traffic conditions